HAL•LEONARD
INSTRUMENTAL
PLAY-ALONG

AUDIO
ACCESS
INCLUDED

PLAYBACK+
Speed • Pitch • Balance • Loop

VIOLA

THE BEATLES

Cover Photo: Fiona Adams/Getty

To access audio visit:
www.halleonard.com/mylibrary
Enter Code
5674-5116-7734-1389

Audio Arrangements by Peter Deneff

ISBN 978-1-4950-9074-5

7777 W. BLUEMOUND RD. P.O. BOX 13819 MILWAUKEE, WI 53213

In Australia Contact:
Hal Leonard Australia Pty. Ltd.
4 Lentara Court
Cheltenham, Victoria, 3192 Australia
Email: ausadmin@halleonard.com.au

Visit Hal Leonard Online at
www.halleonard.com

ALL YOU NEED IS LOVE

VIOLA

Words and Music by JOHN LENNON
and PAUL McCARTNEY

BLACKBIRD

VIOLA

Words and Music by JOHN LENNON
and PAUL McCARTNEY

DAY TRIPPER

VIOLA

Words and Music by JOHN LENNON
and PAUL McCARTNEY

ELEANOR RIGBY

Words and Music by JOHN LENNON
and PAUL McCARTNEY

VIOLA

GET BACK

VIOLA

Words and Music by JOHN LENNON
and PAUL McCARTNEY

HERE, THERE AND EVERYWHERE

VIOLA

Words and Music by JOHN LENNON
and PAUL McCARTNEY

HEY JUDE

VIOLA

Words and Music by JOHN LENNON
and PAUL McCARTNEY

I WILL

VIOLA

Words and Music by JOHN LENNON
and PAUL McCARTNEY

LET IT BE

VIOLA

Words and Music by JOHN LENNON
and PAUL McCARTNEY

LUCY IN THE SKY WITH DIAMONDS

VIOLA

Words and Music by JOHN LENNON
and PAUL McCARTNEY

Moderately

OB-LA-DI, OB-LA-DA

VIOLA

Words and Music by JOHN LENNON
and PAUL McCARTNEY

PENNY LANE

Words and Music by JOHN LENNON
and PAUL McCARTNEY

VIOLA

SOMETHING

VIOLA

Words and Music by
GEORGE HARRISON

TICKET TO RIDE

VIOLA

Words and Music by JOHN LENNON
and PAUL McCARTNEY

YESTERDAY

VIOLA

Words and Music by JOHN LENNON
and PAUL McCARTNEY